Soft Breezes...

paintings & poetry

by Carol Pecoraro

Poetry and art stirs the soul to find truth
and beauty in glimpses of
Divinity in the Universe.

COPYRIGHT © 2013, By Carol Pecoraro

Cover art and Book art by Carol A. Pecoraro

ISBN 978-1484846230

Dedication

I dedicate this book to all who have enlightened, supported and shown love to me.

Special thanks to John Vincent Palozzi, poet, artist and teacher, without whose help this book would not have been published.

Supporters of the Vatican II Council of the Catholic Church especially members of Call To Action

Our Lady of Florida Spiritual Center book club, its members past and present, friends and spiritual travelers.

Dr. Hilda Montalvo, spiritual guide

Rabbi Dr. Rob Lennick and members of Temple Beth Am Havurah

Dr. Sheila Clemon-Karp and women of the Brandeis Women's group

Lifelong friends Carole & Bob Alvino

Faithful friends from Long Island, especially Eileen Curran and Terry & Richard Hughes

Family, especially my many nieces and nephews and
    brother –in-law Vincent Pecoraro and wife, Marie
    brother Richard Humphrey and wife and caretaker, Betty
    sister Jean Cauthorn and her husband Jim
    brother Bill Humphrey and his wife Rosie
    and cousins in the Romano family

Special dedication to my husband, Andrew Pecoraro
    and daughter, Maria Colthorp and
    wonderful son-in-law, Craig Colthorp

Contents

Soft Breezes. . .

Chapter 1

...kiss the cheek

Poems

are meant to be shared

like a mouthwatering meal

on Thanksgiving Day

Awakening

Nature plays with her palette
in the morning sky,

and dips her brush in the bay,

outside my window.

No wonder the birds sing!

Renewal

God in a daffodil,

faithful beauty,

dances, delights.

Wordsworth's pen inspired,

World's worth - restored,

desired.

Haiku

Breeze whispers through the trees
Yellow blooms touch my shoulder

Will I awaken?

Rising sun spills gold -
Shimmering across Lake Worth,
Simple joys enrich!

Joy Spot

In a world full of anxiety,
in a body torn with stress

You are my soul's playmate

my joy spot

my Bach minuet

Joyfilled Prayers

<u>You Winked at Me Today</u>

The breeze kissed my cheek, and
you winked at me today.
I saw it with my inner eye,
your brief glance.
You let me know you saw me there,
and send love.
Then you were silent again.
Only the breeze and I knew
that you winked at me today.

<u>Refreshment</u>

You are my God!
I carry you with me
in my backpack
through . . .the. . .day.
I pause now -
for a drink of joy!

Short verses

My life with you has been a love song
with a new melody every day,

Paisley trees ignite the sky
winter winds whisper
icy frescoes on landscapes

Right now the sun is streaming

through my windows,

and all the bird are out to play.

I wish you violets and birds's song,

and respite for the day.

Play with poetry

Invitation

I called her,
and I called you.
You called her.

Then I called you
and I called her
and I called you.

She called nobody.
Does she want to come?

Carry On

Childhood prank.
Goldfish gone
down the john.
Brother Frank
tells it all.
Wailing wall!
After spank
carry on.
Goldfish gone.
Childhood prank.

Skillet

Sizzling sounds and appealing aromas
Keep this pan in frequent use
Into all hours of the night
Lullabies for indigestion!
Lessons not learned
Early in life, repeat and repeat
Till all the gas is gone.

In Defense of Prepositions

While awesome assertive adjectives may be macabre,
mad or magical even herculean, horrendous and horrible,
nouns and pronouns merely denote,
pedantically or dully, adverbs gloat,
whose job it is to dress the main
VERBS
is where the action is

VERBS!

But, yet, however, conjunctions interject,
the oohs and ahs have it.
Their prize by a neck.

No! Beyond all this, meek prepositions deem,
All the above can only be seen
over, under or in between.
(Though unappreciated, prepositions are needed,
to find the meanings, you see.)

So celebrate verbs. They're impressive. Have might!
But remember to honor the prepositions rights.
As in all of life, the little guy's needed
to lay the ground work, to place.
So you big guys, move over.
Make some room in the clover
for prepositions to stay in the race.

Imagination at Play

"Whee!" said the bee
as he slid down the tree.
Branches browned with honey tea!

Anything can happen behind your eye lid.
Look with a smile, and a picture that hid
will pop up and play like you never did.

Peek beyond your mind's little door.
Breathe, and let your feelings pour
onto a light canvas, not noticed before.

A Toasted Cook

Hail to thee, O leg of Lamb,
And to whence thou came -
my ancient land.
Thou didst inspire Blake's lofty pen,
and moved myself to gaily send
this toast your way in glass of wine -
(as I prepare now such dinner fine) -
chablis to flavor your savored flank,
and fill this cook with liquored prank!

Recipe

Take one anxious person,
Soak in sea's salt
Simmer in sun's smile
Baste with balmy breezes

Remain an hour or two
Till soul is well done.

Share with all;
A flavorful treat
to nourish humanity!

Chapter 2

. . . stir the soul

Ripples of Enlightenment

Formidable bridge of broken cement
dominating the soul path
like the outer level of consciousness
domineering, unyielding,
hiding, but not hindering.

gurgling brook, running freely,
cool, in the shelter of green-leaved fans
breathing gentle newness.
Ripples of enlightenment!

Rushing past in the day's heat
I scrape the crumbling crust.
Later I'll pause here.

The song

. .of the bird calls
me to prayer
Heart and mind dance
to the tune
Thank you, God of
the universe!
I am part of you, and
I sing my song with
the Bird!

Prayer

You call . . .
in stillness

Bird's song speaks . . .

in silence

Stirring my soul

with sunlight

I hear you,

I'll linger here.

Inspired by Wm Blake's poem, " The Tiger"

Femme

Lady in a box can't dance

When the wild
within the tiger's burning
soul springs -
a geyser gift -
rushing toward the sea

    Sophia

        dances freely

           "I am I

             am I

              am!"

When the virgin
sings her unspoiled song, her
sonnet rings - like marriage vows.
Life
blossoms in earth's warm womb
and Sophia dances

    freely.

This Tree's Been Here Before Me

This tree's been here before me.
I, rushing by, claim all I see
from the center of my world
to be judged by me.

(_But this tree's been here before me._)

Who else long gone has sensed its life?
Young brave perhaps shared his belief
in life's sanctity and common bond
for brother sapling, to protect from grief.

Last century's farmer treading by
this shady spot, while searching,
takes its measure for his abode
then leaves behind in forceful lurching.

How many years left, not quite alone,
danced on by squirrel, sung to by birds,
a pheasant here, a rabbit there.
What else before me here's been heard?

Hurricane's thrashing, ice storms sagging
more beautiful now for the beatings taken.
Sudden romantic resting near
feels poetry in her waken.

(I'm just one of many passing through
while these roots and branches
remain unshaken)

I'd love to touch its soul and be as one
(it seems I'm not so central now)
with its days long past and those to come.
I caress its bark and stroke its bough.

This tree's been here before me.

In the Book of Wisdom of theBible, Wisdom (God) is referred to as Sophia,
the feminine word for Wisdom in Greek.

The Dance of Sophia

Dance with us, Sophia!
Let your Spirit move freely
      throughout this room, and throughout this planet.
May your peace and joy be felt by all present here
      as we share with each other what you share with us.
Bless our loved ones and our ministries.
Dance among us, Sophia!
Touch our hearts with compassion
      to listen, and care for all who hunger.
Heal the brokenness in us here,
and in Africa, India, China,
      the Middle East, Central America,
and all places where power abuses.

Dance with us, Sophia!
Fill us with your wisdom
      in this changing world.
Refound your church, Sophia, in your likeness,
that Christ may dance with you in every culture.
Move with us and we will be empowered
      to co-create with you, a resurrected world,
and restore the gifts of creation
      through your love.
Take us by the hand, and heart
      and teach us
      to dance with you, Sophia.

Prayer - two versions

Our Mother

Our Mother
in whom we live.
You are luminous Mystery!
May your relationships thrive,
your will be alive,
among all your offspring,
as it is in your womb.

Nourish us today with your food
      that lasts,
strengthening,
      to let go of what divides,
freeing,
      to become what unites.
and protect us from
      destructive illusions,
for you are the source of
      all life and love

      Amen.

Our Father

Our Father
who art in heaven.
Hallowed be Thy name!
They Kingdom come,
Thy will be done,
On earth
as it is in heaven.

Give us this day our daily bread.
And forgive us our trespasses
as we forgive those who trespass
against us,

And lead us not into temptation,
but deliver us from evil.
For yours is the Kingdom, and
power and glory,
forever and ever.

Amen.

Truth on Trial

Two *grandfathers*
      posturing at a defense table-
    old men, gentle, as in a grocery store
    selecting a ripe melon, the right plantain

Their granddaughters-
    poised behind them,
    educated, lovely -
    oblivious

To *Ghosts* - in the courtroom - unseen
    (and later the jury said, "unheard")
    But the murdered women's families
    huddle heartbroken, hoping for redress

Four godly women - three professed religious and their helper
    stripped by soldiers on the road
    (planned ahead, UN Truth Commission said)
    brutally raped and executed and left
    unclothed by the side of the street,
    dumped like garbage -
    a terror-filled stink of control to
    stifle the vulnerable
    whom the heroines faithfully served.

    The four crucified as their Christ,
    with nods of approval (if not a command) from

Two GENERALS from El Salvador,
    true portraits unveiled in their brutal time -
    a time like a season, returning!
    aided by US State Department - secret providers of
    sanctuary for sadists.

    Today in their testimony they
     wash their hands
     like Pontius Pilate, and say
     by their denials,

      "What is truth?"

Honoring Maryåknoll sisters Maura Clarke and Ita Ford,

Ursuline sister Dorothy Kazel, and

Church worker Jean Donovan,

who dedicated their lives to serving the poor -

Killed in El Salvador December 2, 1980

De Profundis

Screams!
And echoes of screams.
Loved ones -
blown out with windows -
pumping their arms
trying to fly,
grasping for life-
falling -
with rain of steel
and crumbling concrete.
Debris.

Crackling flames
incinerating hopes -
sacrificing,
like pagan rituals,
humanity's best.
Stench of humanity lost
fills the black air
smothering Battery Park,
now battered with ashes.

Twin Towers (of Babel?)
reaching for heights.
(But, oh how we loved them!)
We, like Icarus, flying too high -
tumbling,
returning dust to dust

De Profundis!

I cry out to you, O Lord.
Lord, hear my voice - midst screams
and echoes of screams.

Chapter 3

. . . awaken memories

The Joy of Friendship

(missing our dear friend Marty Curran)
Pick the flowers while they last.
Gather an armful!
Delight in their fleeting fragrance.
Laugh in the sunshine they share.
Alive,
in the joy of friendship!
Too soon a favored one will die,
a special light and fragrance gone.
No longer any color seen
through my heart's overflowing tears.
Bereaved,
by the loss of friendship.
The barren field washes away.
My own color fades.
My petals, too, begin to fall.
Only seeds remain.
Searching,
for life in friendship!
Memories' rich compost becomes fertile soil.
Grace and aires remembered
of such delightful bloom
now brighten my soul's new flowering,
more fragrant, too,
with its recalled perfume.
Sharing,
new expressions of friendship

Diana

Written for Diana Benetti Simone, as she battled with her cancer

I sat with you today in my prayer spot by the green.
A song was raised to heaven then, and **Love** was home, and seen.
His strength invited;
He gently smiled upon bewildered thrall,
as voices took their places in this poor concert hall.
First, **Anguish** cried a silent groan; her figure shrunk in fear.
Ah, **Trust's** gossamer lyric lifted her;
Hope's breeze to linger near.
Pain of heart treads heavy though, as bells so solemn toll,
Bleating, bleeding, beating, (toll)
resounding, pounding, hounding soul.
Flute's fleeting voice of **Peace** is soft, and oft' is hard to hear.
While **Confusion** waves baton to lead,
Pain's shrill chord's too loud and clear.

But **Love** was home and listening as we sat together here,
and silently cried out to Him through chorus of our tears.
Recalling His own Son's same song,
each note He cherished dearly;
"Abba, Father, let this pass.
Yet, your will sees more clearly."

The Son then lent His voice to ours
and Harmony presided.
Resigned were we
to Love's own tune
wherever we may find it.

Grace

(Remembering Grace McCarthy)

Thank you for inviting us

into your home,

your space,

the spaciousness of God.

Your grace-filled hospitality offers

fresh air,

breath of life,

breadth of being;

where self and ego, in mutual love,

dance God's love song

for all the world to see

(remembering Carol Humphrey Pecoraro's Mom)

STANDARD BEARER

Here she sits with that sweet smile
singing with me the kitchen songs my father had sung.
While dinner was cooking,
he'd spin her around the floor as he'd spin his dreams.
What grand schemes!

Here she sits with that sweet smile
recalling with me her work - taking minutes et al.
for bank chiefs meetings -
before rushing home to
     five restless ruffians,
     two nervous pets
     and her aged Irish Mom,
          all clamoring for care.
Dinner for eight held aromas of freshly baked cake
on clean white cloth in the dining room, of course,
as if she'd been home all day.

Here she sits with that sweet smile
eyes not seeing
through her brain's tangled ganglia,
mercifully forgetting the dancing dreamer's straying,
the years of anxious striving
for the perfect standard
she'd thought was needed.   *Mother's eyes twinkled*
                      shining soul in wrinkled face
                         Death turned out the light!

Remembering Dr. Sheila Clemon-Karp of Brandeis' Women's group

Soul Sower
(in the garden of feminine energies)

To what can I liken a valiant woman?
She is like a caretaker in the Queen's favorite garden.
Waking early in the morning
she nurtures the blooms,
loosening the soil to free the roots,
watering them with measured nutrients
till the mind's eye is full
of what emerges as new.

She pours from life's learning
into the pool of reflection
revealing the true feminine
for all who peer in.

As she works, the day's heat
and dry spells don't deter her.
Her own beauty adds color to the palette she sees.
In the face of disease, a new fragrance is breathed.
The scent of endurance perfumes the air
as Valor, a prized blossom, with deep hues, appears.

Seeds from her flower beds spread over the land
surprising the weary with joy-filled new hope.
Some draw near to learn tender secrets.
With generous spirit, her wisdom she shares.

All leave with bouquets
of memories they cherish,
This garden, like Monet's
remembered as prayer.

written in memoriam of Elaine Labriola (Tusinski) Tarbell
Carol's mentor in the Reading Lab of Ward Melville High School

Poetry

A ready smile to greet you
an insightful thought
affirms -
who you are - uncovered!

A quick "hearty" laugh
to temper your steps!

Touch beauty with your spirit
and leave restored.

When the book is closed
you recall its joys
reliving it again and
again.

And so it is with poetry,
we knew as Elaine.

Toast to Mary and Sterling Tremayne

Here's to two people whom God made one!
They bring His love, and with His Son
Spread hope and joy to all they meet.
Their lives have become the finest wheat.

May they live on for all to see;
The Kingdom is here.
They hold a key!

Made in the USA
Lexington, KY
21 May 2013